NEW YORK
GIANTS

SportsZone

An Imprint of Abdo Publishing
abdopublishing.com

BY SAULIE BLUMBERG

abdopublishing.com

Published by Abdo Publishing, a division of ABDO, PO Box 398166, Minneapolis, Minnesota 55439. Copyright © 2017 by Abdo Consulting Group, Inc. International copyrights reserved in all countries. No part of this book may be reproduced in any form without written permission from the publisher. SportsZone™ is a trademark and logo of Abdo Publishing.

Printed in the United States of America, North Mankato, Minnesota
042016
092016

Cover Photo: Evan Pinkus/AP Images
Interior Photos: Evan Pinkus/AP Images, 1; Charlie Riedel/AP Images, 4-5; Elaine Thompson/AP Images, 6; Dick Druckman/AP Images, 7; Pro Football Hall of Fame/AP Images, 8-9, 10-11; Harry Harris/AP Images, 12-13; Ruben Goldberg/AP Images, 14-15; AP Images, 16-17, 22-23; G. Paul Burnett/AP Images, 18-19; Kathy Kmonicek/AP Images, 20; Al Messerschmidt/AP Images, 21, 24; NFL Photos/AP Images, 25; Matt Slocum/AP Images, 26-27; Julio Cortez/AP Images, 28; David Stluka/AP Images, 29

Editor: Patrick Donnelly
Series Designer: Nikki Farinella

Cataloging-in-Publication Data
Names: Blumberg, Saulie, author.
Title: New York Giants / by Saulie Blumberg.
Description: Minneapolis, MN : Abdo Publishing, [2017] | Series: NFL up close |
    Includes index.
Identifiers: LCCN 2015960438 | ISBN 9781680782264 (lib. bdg.) |
    ISBN 9781680776379 (ebook)
Subjects: LCSH: New York Giants (Football team)--History--Juvenile
    literature. | National Football League--Juvenile literature. | Football--Juvenile
    literature. | Professional sports--Juvenile literature. | Football teams--
    New York--Juvenile literature.
Classification: DDC 796.332--dc23
LC record available at http://lccn.loc.gov/2015960438

TABLE OF CONTENTS

TYREE'S MIRACLE

The New York Giants were in trouble. They were losing to the New England Patriots by four points late in the Super Bowl. The Patriots had not lost a game the entire 2007 season. They were a few minutes away from making history. The Giants needed something special to stop it from happening.

Nobody thought David Tyree would be the one to deliver the big play. Tyree was buried on the wide receiver depth chart. He was mainly used on special teams. He had made only four catches in the 2007 season.

FAST FACT

After the Super Bowl, David Tyree caught only four more passes the rest of his career. He retired in 2009.

Giants quarterback Eli Manning tries to escape the New England Patriots' pass rush late in the Super Bowl on February 3, 2008.

Quarterback Eli Manning dropped back to pass. Patriots defenders zeroed in on him. They had him in their grasp. But Manning twisted away from the rush and heaved the ball downfield. Tyree leaped high over star safety Rodney Harrison. Tyree pinned the ball against his helmet with his right hand as he fell. He held on for a 32-yard gain with 59 seconds left.

Moments later, wide receiver Plaxico Burress caught a much more routine 13-yard pass for the game-winning touchdown. The Patriots were no longer undefeated, and the Giants were Super Bowl champions with a 17-14 victory.

David Tyree, *left*, pins the ball to his helmet as Rodney Harrison tries to knock it away.

Plaxico Burress hauls in the game-winning touchdown pass as the Giants shock the Patriots in the Super Bowl.

FAST FACT

The Giants ruined New England's perfect season. That left the 1972 Miami Dolphins as the only undefeated champions in the Super Bowl era.

Members of the first New York Giants team pose for a photo in 1925.

THE SNEAKERS GAME

The New York Giants have been around almost as long as the National Football League (NFL) itself. They started playing in 1925, and they won their first NFL championship two years later. That was the start of a great era of Giants football. They played for the league title nine times in 20 years. They are probably best remembered for a championship they played under unusual circumstances.

Steve Owen coached the Giants for 23 years (1931–1953). He retired with a team-record 151 victories.

The Giants wrap up Bears fullback Bronko Nagurski in the 1934 NFL Championship Game, also called the "Sneakers Game."

The Giants' home field was an icy mess for the 1934 NFL Championship Game against the Chicago Bears. Chicago led 10-3 at halftime. New York's players were slipping all over the field. But Giants coach Steve Owen had an idea. He had basketball sneakers delivered from a nearby college. In the second half, the Giants wore the rubber-soled shoes.

Suddenly, even though the turf had gotten more slippery, the Giants were no longer losing their footing. New York outscored the Bears 27-0 in the fourth quarter. Ken Strong's 42-yard touchdown run put the Giants ahead to stay. New York won 30-13.

GLORY DAYS

The Giants won the NFL title again in 1938, but they won it only one more time in the next 48 years. Still, they had some strong teams, especially from 1956 to 1963. They won 73 of 102 games in that eight-year stretch. They won the NFL championship in 1956. Then they had a remarkable streak of five runner-up finishes in six years.

New York lost the championship game against the Baltimore Colts in 1958 and 1959. The Green Bay Packers beat them in 1961 and 1962. And the Chicago Bears edged them in 1963.

Giants running back Mel Triplett, *center*, blows past two Bears and bowls over an official on the way to the end zone during New York's 47-7 victory in the 1956 NFL Championship Game.

In that era, the NFL was growing more popular with fans around the United States. Those Giants teams and their big stars played a large part in that growth. Many of the players are now members of the Pro Football Hall of Fame. Frank Gifford played both halfback and receiver for the Giants and was a four-time All-Pro. He retired in 1964 and became a famous TV announcer. Quarterback Y. A. Tittle was the NFL Most Valuable Player (MVP) in 1963. Linebacker Sam Huff anchored the defense for eight seasons.

Giants quarterback Y. A. Tittle flings a pass against the Dallas Cowboys during his MVP season.

THE FUMBLE

After losing the 1963 NFL Championship Game, the Giants had some lean years. They did not even reach the playoffs again until 1981. One game in particular became a symbol of that dark era. Giants fans refer to it as "The Fumble."

In 1978, the Giants led the Philadelphia Eagles 17-12. New York had the ball late in the game. The Eagles could not stop the clock. All the Giants had to do was take a knee and the game would be over.

The Giants began playing their home games in New Jersey with the opening of Giants Stadium in 1976.

16

The Giants played their home games in two baseball stadiums in their early years: the Polo Grounds from 1925 to 1955, and Yankee Stadium from 1956 to 1973.

GIANTS

GIANTS STADIUM

Joe Pisarcik, *bottom*, can only watch as Herman Edwards picks up his untimely fumble and returns it for the game-winning touchdown on November 19, 1978.

Instead, the Giants' coaches called a running play. Quarterback Joe Pisarcik turned to hand off to fullback Larry Csonka. But Csonka never got the ball. It bounced right to Eagles cornerback Herman Edwards. He scooped up the fumble and ran into the end zone for a 26-yard touchdown.

Philadelphia's shocking 19-17 victory sent the Giants tumbling to their sixth straight losing season. The streak reached eight years, but then a rookie linebacker changed the NFL and the Giants' fortunes in 1981.

19

LT AND THE TUNA

In 1981, the Giants used the second pick in the NFL Draft on linebacker Lawrence Taylor. Taylor had an immediate impact. He was a first-team All-Pro selection eight times in his first nine seasons. He was the NFL MVP in 1986. The Giants made the playoffs in Taylor's rookie season. And better times were to come.

Taylor was fast, strong, and intense. He was best known for sacking the quarterback. Few players ever did it better.

Lawrence Taylor smothers a Kansas City Chiefs running back in 1984.

Lawrence Taylor, *left*, pressured the quarterback better than anybody else in his era.

FAST FACT

Lawrence Taylor had 132.5 official quarterback sacks in his career. He led the NFL with 20.5 sacks in 1986.

FAST FACT

Bill Parcells had a 77-49-1 record with the Giants. They went 14-2 and 13-3 in his two Super Bowl-winning seasons.

But Taylor could not do it all by himself. In 1983, the Giants hired Bill Parcells as their coach. Parcells was called "Tuna" because of his resemblance to a cartoon tuna from a popular TV commercial. But his defenses were no laughing matter.

Linebackers Harry Carson and Carl Banks teamed with Taylor to dominate opposing offenses. Those Giants teams had simple but effective offensive plans. Quarterback Phil Simms took care of the ball. The ground game chewed up the clock. And more often than not, the Giants would win a low-scoring game.

Coach Bill Parcells, *center*, gives instruction to quarterback Phil Simms in 1984.

In 1986, Parcells and the Giants reached their first Super Bowl. Simms completed 22 of 25 passes for 268 yards and three touchdowns. Defensive end Leonard Marshall had two of New York's four sacks. The Giants routed Denver 39-20.

Four years later, the Giants were back. This time, they were underdogs against the Buffalo Bills. But Parcells and his staff put together a great game plan. The Giants controlled the ball for more than 40 minutes—almost three quarters of the game. That kept Buffalo's high-flying offense off the field. New York pulled off a 20-19 upset.

Linebacker Harry Carson dumps the contents of a Gatorade bucket on Bill Parcells at the end of the Giants' defeat of Denver in the Super Bowl.

Giants players celebrate after knocking off the Buffalo Bills to win the Super Bowl for the second time in four years.

FAST FACT

Harry Carson is credited with popularizing the now-traditional Gatorade shower that winning coaches often receive on the sidelines. He started dousing Bill Parcells during the 1986 season.

ELITE ELI

The San Diego Chargers made Eli Manning the first player chosen in the 2004 NFL Draft. But a few minutes later, the Chargers traded Manning to the Giants, and a new era began in New York.

After backing up Kurt Warner for nine games that season, Manning took over as the starter. He learned on the job. In January 2008, he led the Giants to three road wins in the playoffs. Then he guided them past the undefeated Patriots in the Super Bowl.

Eli Manning drops back to pass in a playoff victory over the Dallas Cowboys on January 13, 2008.

FAST FACT

Eli Manning's older brother, Peyton Manning, is the NFL's only five-time MVP. Their father, Archie Manning, played 14 seasons in the NFL.

Four years later, Manning and the Giants did it again. They trailed the Patriots in the final minute of the Super Bowl. But running back Ahmad Bradshaw scampered into the end zone from 6 yards out. New York held on for a 21-17 victory.

The Giants missed the playoffs the next four years. But a new star emerged in wide receiver Odell Beckham Jr. One of the most exciting players in the NFL gave Giants fans something to look forward to in the future.

Odell Beckham Jr. hauls in a touchdown pass against Washington in 2014.

Ahmad Bradshaw cuts through the Patriots defense to score the winning touchdown in the Giants' second Super Bowl victory over New England.

TIMELINE

1925
Businessman Tim Mara buys an NFL team for $500 and names it the Giants.

1927
The Giants go 11-1-1 and win the NFL Championship, giving up only 20 points all season.

1934
On a frozen Polo Grounds field, the Giants put on sneakers at halftime and upset the undefeated Bears 30-13 to win another championship.

1938
Hank Soar's 23-yard touchdown catch gives the Giants a 23-17 victory over Green Bay and a third NFL title.

1956
The Giants beat the Bears 47-7 to cap their first season in Yankee Stadium with an NFL title.

1958
In the NFL's first overtime contest, often called "The Greatest Game Ever Played," the Giants fall to Johnny Unitas and the Baltimore Colts 23-17 in the NFL Championship Game.

1987
On January 25, the Giants win their first Super Bowl, defeating the Denver Broncos 39-20. Quarterback Phil Simms is named the game's MVP.

2008
On February 3, the Giants ruin New England's perfect season with a 17-14 win in the Super Bowl.

2012
On February 5, quarterback Eli Manning and coach Tom Coughlin lead the Giants to another Super Bowl win against the Patriots, 21-17.

GLOSSARY

ALL-PRO
A player voted as the best in the NFL at his position in a season.

DEPTH CHART
A list of starting and backup players at a position.

ELITE
Among the best at something.

FUMBLE
When a player with the ball loses possession, allowing the opponent a chance to recover it.

PLAYOFFS
A set of games after the regular season that decides which team will be the champion.

SACK
A tackle of the quarterback behind the line of scrimmage before he can pass the ball.

SPECIAL TEAMS
The players on the field during punts, kickoffs, field goals, and extra-point kicks.

UPSET
When a supposedly weaker team beats a stronger team.

INDEX

ABOUT THE AUTHOR

Saulie Blumberg is a New York resident who is studying to become a physician. He has also authored numerous sports books for young readers. He considers himself an expert on nearly every sport, particularly football.